Keanu Reeves

Julia Holt

Published in association with The Basic Skills Agency

Hodder & Stoughton

A MEMBER OF THE HODDER HEADLINE GROUP

Acknowledgements
Cover: © Camera Press
Photos: p. iv © London features; pp. 7, 12, 16, 23, 25 The Kobal Collection.

Every effort has been made to trace copyright holders of material reproduced in this book. Any rights not acknowledged will be acknowledged in subsequent printings if notice is given to the publisher.

Orders: please contact Bookpoint Ltd, 130 Milton Park, Abingdon, Oxon OX14 4SB. Telephone: (44) 01235 827720, Fax: (44) 01235 400454. Lines are open from 9.00 – 6.00, Monday to Saturday, with a 24 hour message answering service. Email address: orders@bookpoint.co.uk

British Library Cataloguing in Publication Data
A catalogue record for this title is available from The British Library

ISBN 0 340 84881 2

Second edition. First published 1997
Impression number 10 9 8 7 6 5 4 3 2 1
Year   2007 2006 2005 2004 2003 2002

Copyright © 2002 Julia Holt

Typeset by SX Composing DTP, Rayleigh, Essex.
Printed in Great Britain for Hodder & Stoughton Educational, a division of Hodder Headline Plc, 338 Euston Road, London NW1 3BH by The Bath Press Ltd.

Contents

Keanu rides his 1974 Norton
motorbike.

1 Why is Keanu Reeves a Star?

He turns down parts in big films
to act on the stage
or to play in his band Dog Star.
Some of the films are not smash hits.
He doesn't go to Hollywood parties.
He doesn't want to be a star.
He has even said,
'I don't want to be super famous.'

Keanu doesn't own a flashy house or car.
He lives in hotels and rides a 1974
Norton Combat Commando motorbike.

Maybe his fans love him because of this.
Because he is ordinary and different
at the same time.
It is hard to say what kind of person he is.
He is not easy to pin down.

2 Early Years

Even Keanu's childhood years
were a mixture of ordinary and different.

His mother is English.
His father is half-Hawaiian and half-Chinese.

Keanu was born in Lebanon
on 2 September 1964.
He was given a Hawaiian name.
It means 'the coolness'.

His parents split up
when Keanu and his sister Kim were little.
His mother, Patric,
took her children to New York.
She married a film director called Paul.
The family went to live in Canada.
Keanu and Kim went to school there.
Keanu became a Canadian citizen
and he still is to this day.

Patric and Paul split up a year later.
But Keanu always stayed in touch
with his step-father Paul.

Patric went on to marry twice more
and to have another baby called Karina.
Each time a new man
came into his mother's life,
the family moved.
Keanu changed school almost every year.
He was dyslexic and left-handed.
School was very difficult for him.
In the end, Keanu dropped out, aged 17.
He sharpened skates and made pasta for a living.

His mother made clothes
for the rich and famous stars.
So Keanu was used to seeing famous people,
like David Bowie and Alice Cooper.

Keanu's childhood was very different
from other kids' lives,
but he also did ordinary things.
He loved playing ice hockey.
He was so good in goal
that his nickname was 'The Wall'.

3 First Films

Keanu had another interest,
which was acting.

He acted in school plays.
In the holidays he flew to LA
to stay with his step-father Paul.
He hung around on film sets
as his step-father worked.

Back in Canada
Keanu changed school again.
This time he went to an acting school.
He went straight into the top class.

The school did a show in 1983.
An agent saw the 18 year-old Keanu.
She signed him up.
She got him lots of work
doing TV adverts.

Keanu liked to be scruffy.
His agent tried to make him smarter.
It didn't work.
But it didn't matter.
He still got the parts.

In 1984 he got his first small film part.
He played an ice hockey player
in a comedy film called *Young Blood*.

It was an awful film
but at least it was a start for Keanu.

In the spring of the next year
Keanu was chosen to be in a Disney film.
He went to LA for the film *Young Again*.
The film industry in Canada
was small, at that time.
There wasn't much work.

Keanu drove to LA
in his 20 year-old Volvo car.
This time it wasn't a holiday.
This time he stayed.

At first he lived with his step-father Paul.
Then he got himself a new agent
and rented a flat.

Keanu got parts in TV films.
But he wanted to do more
than just TV work.

He got a part in the film *River's Edge*.
It's the film of a true story.
The murder of a young girl.
The film showed the dark side of America.

It was a surprise hit
and the critics liked Keanu.

In 1987 in Hollywood,
there was a big casting call.
A film company was making a film
called *Bill and Ted's Excellent Adventure*.
They were looking for actors.

Many actors wanted to be in this film.
In the end Keanu and Alex Winter
were chosen.

Keanu and Alex Winter in *Bill and Ted's Excellent Adventure.*

The film was a comedy
about two school kids, Bill and Ted.
Keanu played Ted.
The kids are no good at history lessons.
But they are given
a time-travel machine to help them.

Bill and Ted go back in time.
They bring back famous people
to help them with their history homework.

The critics didn't like the film.
But it was a box office success.
It made a lot of money
and it made Keanu a star.

Some of Bill and Ted's words from the film
were used by young people
all over the world.
Words like 'bogus', 'dude'
and 'most excellent'.

4   Type-cast

Keanu was in hospital
when he found out that he had a small part
in *Dangerous Liaisons*.
He had crashed his motorbike in LA.
He was riding in a canyon at night
without any lights.
He has a long scar
from his chest to his navel
where they had to take out his spleen.

Dangerous Liaisons is a costume drama.
It's a film about sex, power and money.
Keanu plays a young man
who is used by others
as part of their cruel games.

Keanu was unhappy with his acting.
The critics said he looked out of place.
It was proving difficult for him
to get away from playing 'dudes'.
He was worried he was getting type-cast.

He tried to get away
from playing a dude again in 1989.
He played a hit man
in the film *I Love You To Death*.
On the film set he met a new friend.
His name was River Phoenix.
They were good friends
for the next six years.

5 Taking Off

In 1990, when he was 25,
Keanu's career began to take off.
He made three films in seven months.
The first was a thriller called *Point Break*.
He played an FBI agent,
the same age as himself.
Point Break took 77 days to make
and it was a big success when it came out.

Then Keanu flew to Oregon
to make *My Own Private Idaho*.
Keanu made this film with his friend
River Phoenix.
They played rent boys.

It was a difficult film for both actors.
But they enjoyed working together.
Today the film is called a classic.

Keanu with River Phoenix in *My Own Private Idaho*.

6   Hard Work

By now Keanu was very tired.
He went on to make another Bill and Ted film.
He kept his hair long to hide his tired eyes.
The film was supposed to be a blockbuster.
It wasn't – it was a bit of a flop.

Keanu didn't rest.
He rushed into making *Dracula*.
But he was lifeless in the film.
The critics said that he looked
as though he'd lost all his blood
before the film started.
So he took a rest and didn't work
until the next year, 1992.

His next film was made in Italy.
It was a Shakespeare play
called *Much Ado About Nothing*.
Keanu played Don John.
He is the strong silent type
and he makes problems for everyone.

The film was a box office hit.
It made $48 million worldwide.

In that same year
Keanu also made *The Little Buddha*.
He played a young prince
who has never left his home.
He doesn't know the meaning
of old age or sickness.

At the age of 29,
the prince leaves home to travel and learn.
The prince becomes The Buddha.

The film was made
in America, Bhutan and Nepal.
Keanu loved being in Bhutan.
He felt free, no one knew him.

In the film,
Keanu changed his looks many times.
For the part of the story
when The Buddha fasted,
Keanu ate nothing but oranges.
He got very thin.

7   Success and Sadness

Keanu had great success
and great sadness in 1993.
It was a big year for him.

In the film *Speed*
Keanu played a SWAT agent.
(SWAT is short for
Special Weapons and Technical unit.)

The story takes place on a speeding bus.
If the bus's speed drops below 50 mph
then the bus blows up.
The SWAT agent has to save the day.

Eight weeks into filming
River Phoenix died from a drugs overdose.
The news hit Keanu very hard.

Keanu had great success in the film, *Speed*.

Speed was a big success.
It made $330 million worldwide.
Keanu had finally got rid of Ted.

Just as the film came out
Keanu's father was sent to jail
for possession of drugs.
If he was angry with his father before,
he was even angrier with him now.

Keanu ended the year
by joining a rock band.
He played bass with Dog Star.
The band keeps his feet on the ground.

8 Film Flops

Keanu's next film was a big flop.
It was called
Johnny Mnemonic.

A mnemonic is a special way
to remember things.
It's like a jingle.
Keanu played a man
who could remember electronic data
because he had a micro-chip
in his head.

The critics said that the film was
flatter than a floppy disc!

Next Keanu chose to appear in a drama.
It was to be his first romantic drama.
The film was called *A Walk in the Clouds*.

He played a GI
coming home from World War II.
He agrees to pose as the husband
of a pregnant woman,
who he meets on a bus.

In the film they go back
to her family in California.
Then the GI really falls in love with her.

When it came out in 1995 the critics said
it was sweet and old-fashioned.
But it was not a blockbuster.

It seemed like Keanu's career
was going downhill.
He didn't have an Oscar.
He wasn't a method actor
like the others in his age group.
In fact he wasn't like the others at all.

In the summer of 1995
he took off with his band, Dog Star.
They did tours of Japan and America.
This was a rest from films for Keanu.

Keanu playing in his band, Dog Star.

9   Moving On

Keanu's next move made Hollywood angry.
He was asked to work on *Speed 2*,
but he didn't like the script.
He turned down $11 million
and went back to Canada
to play Hamlet on stage.
Everyone said that Keanu was mad.
But *Speed 2* was a flop.
Then people said
that he really was very smart.

Keanu had put on weight on his Dog Star tour.
He had to lose it
for his part in *Chain Reaction*.
It's a big action film.
The story starts with a big explosion
in a science lab.
Keanu is a scientist and he gets away
from the explosion on a motorbike.

In 1996, Keanu had another motorbike crash.
He ran into a car in LA and broke his ankle.
He said that his stunt work in *Chain Reaction*
stopped him from being hurt even more.

When Keanu saw the script
for *The Devil's Advocate*, he knew it was good.
Plus, he wanted to work with Al Pacino.

So after making a CD with Dog Star,
he started work on *The Devil's Advocate*.
In the film Keanu played
a young lawyer from Florida.
He is head-hunted
by a powerful New York law firm.

He goes to New York.
But he finds out that his boss,
played by Al Pacino, is the devil.
The devil offers the young lawyer
anything that he wants.
What will he do?

It's a good story with an exciting twist at the end.
Keanu was on the way up again.

Keanu got to work with Al Pacino in *The Devil's Advocate*.

Then Keanu was off to Australia.
Not to make a film
but to get ready to make a film.
He spent four months learning Kung Fu
and how to act when hanging from wires.

The film he was getting ready for
was *The Matrix*.
It was an all-action blockbuster.

The Matrix is a sci-fi film.
It's the story of Neo,
a computer hacker.

Neo is chosen as the leader
of an underground gang.
They know that the world
people see is a sham.
They want to free people
and show them the truth.

The Matrix took a year to make.
When it came out in 1999
it was a huge success.
It was Keanu's biggest hit so far
and it made him a top star.

Keanu in the all-action blockbuster, *The Matrix*.

10 Tragedy

The end of 1999
was also a sad time for Keanu.
His girlfriend, Jennifer, was pregnant.
But the baby was still-born.
The death nearly made the couple split up.
They were both very sad.

Keanu threw himself into work.
In 2000, apart from a new Dog Star album,
he made three films.

One was a comedy.
It was called *The Replacements*.
Keanu had to put on weight
to play the washed-up footballer.
He gets a second chance to play
when the other players go on strike.

The training for the film was very hard.
He kept ice packs in his fridge
to put on his knees after a day on the set.

After playing two violent men
in *The Gift* and *The Watcher*,
Keanu was looking for a romantic part.

He chose the film *Sweet November*.
It's the story of a young woman.
She chooses a new boyfriend every month
and she helps them to be better people.
Keanu is chosen for November.
But he is not sure
that he needs to be a better person.
Then he finds out
that the girl has a tragic secret.

Then, in April 2001,
tragedy struck Keanu again.
His 29 year-old girlfriend, Jennifer,
was killed in a car crash.
She had never come to terms
with the death of their baby.
Keanu was heartbroken.

11 The Future

Just before Jennifer died, Keanu had
started work on the next two *Matrix* films.

After the funeral he flew to Australia
to carry on working.
The two movies are being filmed back to back.
It will take a year to finish both.
Again, the training will be hard.

The stories are a big secret
but some of the actors from the first film
will be in the next two.
Keanu plays Neo again.
He will get $30 million for the two films.

But Keanu says:
'Money doesn't buy you happiness
but it does buy you the freedom
to live your life the way you want to.'

And that's just what he does.